PLANNED GIVING

How to Ask for
Transformational Legacy Gifts

Rob Henson, CFRE

PLANNED GIVING
How to Ask for Transformational Legacy Gifts

iUniverse books may be ordered through booksellers or by contacting:

iUniverse
1663 Liberty Drive
Bloomington, IN 47403
www.iuniverse.com
1-800-Authors (1-800-288-4677)

ISBN: 978-1-5320-0008-9 (sc)
ISBN: 978-1-5320-0009-6 (e)

Library of Congress Control Number: 2016909570

Print information available on the last page.

iUniverse rev. date: 02/01/2017

DEDICATION

To my grandmother, Sarah Henson-Hill. She is my
first and biggest fan. She has guided me and our family
with elegance, wit, grace, and an abundance of love.

CONTENTS

ACKNOWLEDGEMENTS

First, and foremost, I want to thank my wife, Heather. She loves, inspires, and challenges me. She has the best strategic mind I have ever encountered and is the most loving and loyal partner I could hope for.

I would also like to thank several people without whom this book would not be possible:

Maura Robinson for telling me over lunch that I have a book to write and challenging me to get to it.

Rev. Msgr. Ken Knapp who guided me on the path of stewardship and development many years ago.

Bentley Foster and Dan Conway who helped me transition from a staff development officer to a national consultant.

Perry Hammock and Tom Monaghan who are brothers in fundraising who generously share their wisdom with me.

INTRODUCTION

I remember so much about the day I asked for my first
planned gift. I will never forget how cold it was outside and
how nervous I was. There was a light rain and the holidays
were just around the corner. I got to the meeting early
so I could get settled. I reviewed my talking points and
wondered how this conversation would end. I didn't have
any formal preparation for this moment. This was early in
my fundraising career. The events of that day were about to
change my career and my life forever.

The donor was ready to make a transformational gift.
I knew that this day could change the future for hundreds
of people in our community. The weight of that lay on my
shoulders. I was just a newbie. What if I made a mistake?
Throughout the rest of this book, I will bring you along
in my relationship with the donor and tell you how the
meeting ended!

When I reflect on that day, I wish I had owned a book
like this. In those days, becoming a fundraising professional
was really more like an apprenticeship but without any
formalized progression (though today there are several
degrees in nonprofit management and philanthropy). I
had great coaching and advice to get ready for that donor

meeting. Having a book to guide me through the entire process would have really helped. It would have been helpful to have everything I needed in a complete resource guide which is why I have written this book for you!

There are several books on planned giving from the very simple to the extremely complex. *This book is designed for nonprofits that would like to start their first planned giving program.* It can also be a handy resource for those nonprofits that have tried planned giving, but were disappointed by their results.

About a week into a new fundraising role, I was charged with starting a planned giving program. I searched online for all the relevant planned giving books. I talked with expert advisers and I was totally overwhelmed. I was overwhelmed by the complexity of the material. I was overwhelmed by the knowledge of the experts. I was overwhelmed by how technical the gifts could be in their construction.

In the beginning, what I really needed was a book to teach me how to find and reach planned gift donors. My hope is that this book will help you as you begin developing a planned giving program for your nonprofit. It contains all the information that I wish I had a couple of years ago plus a few nuggets that are new.

Another reason I wrote this book is because I believe every nonprofit should have access to clear, relevant, and practical strategies for planned giving. It can be easy to believe that only institutions that are very large, have a big national footprint, have a planned giving officer, or a planned giving department have any business being involved in the field of planned giving. That's just not true.

It can be easy for a nonprofit to believe that they don't have the time or the staff to be involved in planned giving. Every nonprofit no matter the size, how long you've been around, or how many staff you have can be involved in the wonderful field of planned giving! Planned giving shouldn't be only accessible as a fundraising tool to the largest, most complex and well-staffed organizations. Planned giving strategies should be available to any nonprofit that wants to offer their donors a way of making a legacy gift. Part of the purpose of this book is to make sure that we level the playing field for all nonprofits to be a part of this very important perspective in philanthropy.

Lastly, I'm writing this book is because of the opportunity available as a result of the retirement of the baby boomer generation. In some texts, you'll see this referred to as the "silver tsunami" or the "grey wave". About ten thousand boomers are retiring every day and transitioning into the next phase of their life. Current research tells us that baby boomers will live longer, be healthier, and be more active in volunteer work than any generation before them. Research also indicates that boomers are going to be retiring with forty trillion dollars in assets. That number is sometimes estimated to be as low as eight trillion and even as high as sixty! No matter the final amount, a sizable chunk of that asset pool will be transferred to their heirs and nonprofits. It is well known today that there are not enough development officers staffing our nonprofits to be able to handle the needs of this baby boomer generation and their charitable interests. Part of the reason for writing this book is to help all nonprofits be able to invite the participation and support of boomers in a way that honors their charitable interest, and continues the vital mission of the nonprofit community in the United States.

There is a quote that has inspired me over the years by Dr. Martin Luther King, "You must take the first step in faith. You don't have to see the whole staircase." In my nonprofit experience, it seems that we have a hard time committing to a new revenue stream. Planned giving seems to be a field of fundraising that looks overly complicated and time consuming. In fairness, there are complex aspects of planned giving and some of the gift types can be complex. By just committing to starting a program with the simplest gift types and the most basic outreach strategies, I believe all nonprofits can be successful in planned giving. I have written this book in hopes that it provides enough tools so that nonprofits can take that first step in planned giving. This book explains the first steps in planned giving. There are many more steps in the staircase. There are many more types of planned gifts than we can cover in this book. We can climb the rest of the staircase over time.

This book refers to concepts in law, accounting, and financial services. This book is not intended to provide legal, accounting, or financial planning advice. This book is for education purposes only. Donors should seek the counsel of licensed experts when planning their legacy gifts.

CHAPTER 1

The Five Characteristics
of Planned Giving

Over the years, I have found there are many misconceptions about planned giving. Some are minor, but others are more significant. Before we attempt to define planned giving by what it is, let's take a moment to define planned giving by what it is not.

First, planned giving is not complicated. There is a tendency in the planned giving world to use a great deal of ink *on the most complex gift available* in the planned giving toolbox. I guess this helps some people feel very smart. Unfortunately, this makes the process look more difficult than it needs to be. It can intimidate organizations from getting involved in planned giving. This does not have to be a complicated endeavor. It is an opportunity to offer a donor a way of making a legacy gift that will impact a nonprofit organization after the death of the donor. It also has the potential to impact the nonprofit during the life of the donor as well. A variety of tools are available to donors to make a charitable gift through planned giving. The ones that are most commonly used are the ones that are the most simple. Later in this book, I will show three of the easiest and most common types of planned gifts that any nonprofit can offer their donors.

Second, planned giving is not just for big organizations. Often, the larger the organization, the more staff and resources they have dedicated to planned giving. You'll see entire websites that nonprofits have built around their planned giving endeavors. All of this gives the appearance that dedicated staff and infrastructure are necessary to pursue planned giving opportunities. While helpful, you don't have to have a big staff to get started. Even the small nonprofit can pursue planned gifts.

Planned giving programs can be developed by organizations of any size. All nonprofits can be a part of this form of philanthropy, whether you have a marketing director who is sharing responsibility with development, or a CEO who is dedicating some portion of their time to development, or if you have a full-time development officer who's balancing grants, annual funds, events and major gifts. There is a way for all organizations regardless of their size to offer this form of charitable support to their donor base.

Third, planned giving isn't just for financial experts. I concluded (quite wrongly) early in my planned giving career that only CPAs and lawyers could be involved in planned giving. Thankfully, one of my mentors advised me otherwise and I now know that as a development officer, it is my job to seek out planned gifts. The lawyers, CPAs and wealth advisers become your allies. They should populate your planned giving committees. They should be your mentors.

It's not required that you be trained in those fields. Your role is to begin a conversation with your donor about making a legacy gift. Over time, you steward that conversation to a point where you can then include experts. Together, you all structure a gift that help the donor make a lasting impact. Your allies and mentors have the tools to make a donor's planned gift into a reality.

With some basic tools and advice, *all* nonprofits and their development staff can and should be involved in this important stream of philanthropy. You have the responsibility, as a steward of your donor's care for your nonprofit, to ask for these types of gifts. Yes, these gifts require more technical know-how than your typical annual or capital campaign gift, but this is where your board and volunteers come in. By taking a careful look at the members of your board and volunteers, you will likely find they have the expertise to help craft the planned gift documents. They are on the board because they care about your nonprofit and when they find out their expertise is needed and appreciated in more ways than in just the board meetings, they will be happy and likely honored to help you!

Planned Giving Defined

Now that we have discussed what planned giving is not, let's define planned giving for the modern nonprofit. *Planned giving is about relationships.* It is a special moment. You are able to create an opportunity for a donor to make a lasting impact on your organization. If you understand the needs of your donor and match those needs with the mission of your organization, you are well on your way to creating a planned giving program.

In the field of planned giving there are probably more definitions of planned giving than there are actual ways to make planned gifts! That's because there's a lot of dynamic change happening in the field of planned giving. I have heard this type of giving called legacy giving, gift planning, and Kingdom giving. For ease of use, we will settle on the term "planned giving" for this text.

We have more planned giving prospects today than there have ever been. There is more wealth about to be transferred to nonprofits and the next generation of heirs than there even has been before. That means there's a lot of fluctuation in the planned giving market, both between the people who will make planned gifts and the organizations that intend to receive them.

For the purpose of our journey together, we will begin with a commonly accepted definition of planned giving from the Association of Fundraising Professionals. According to the AFP,

> a planned gift is a systematic effort to identify and cultivate a person for the purpose of generating a major gift that is structured and that integrates sound personal, financial, and estate planning concepts with the prospect's plans for lifetime or testamentary giving. A planned gift has tax implications and is often transmitted through a legal instrument such as a will or trust.

It will be helpful for us to break down that definition into five key components. First of all, a planned gift is *personal*. This separates planned giving from gifts that come from corporations and foundations. Those gifts generally come from an application process and are made by entities that don't have estate plans. Planned gifts are always personal because they involve the donor who intends to leave some part of their estate to a nonprofit. It is personal because a gift officer representing the organization has cultivated and solicited the gift. This gift is the result of a relationship that has been cultivated and stewarded.

However, just because it is personal, that shouldn't lead us to believe that this is a one-on-one relationship. Planned gifts often involve the input of family, financial advisors, legal advisors, and other influencers in the donor's sphere. It's important to remember that as we cultivate planned gifts, while we are asking for the gift from a person, there may be several people who are involved in making the final decision. Gift officers are well advised to build relationships in these other professional categories as you will likely encounter these advisors at some point when working with a donor. Also, in the best of circumstances, these advisors can become a gift referral source for you when their clients have charitable interests.

Another key characteristic is that a planned gift is *structured*. These gifts are the result of a donor stating that some part of their estate has a charitable purpose. The way the donor states that purpose usually has significant structural components. These components may involve how a person gives through a will or a trust. They may involve the transference of a business or property to a nonprofit.

These structures require expert counsel for the donor and the nonprofit. Structural components also include how the gift might be used. When we receive gifts to the annual fund or special appeals, those gifts tend to be unrestricted to "highest and best use", while planned gifts are sometimes restricted to particular purposes.

The third component is that there are *tax implications* involved. In the reformation of tax codes in the 1980s, planned giving became more popular as a way of preserving assets and reducing tax burden for donors. This means that many planned gifts have significant tax impact for donors, their heirs, and the organizations that will receive their gifts. Relief from taxes does not seem to be a primary motivator for donors to make a planned gift. However, it is important to consider the current life and after death tax implications of the donor's gift. Because of that, you will need to have tax advisors on the board of your nonprofit and you will often be interfacing with the tax advisors of your donor so that the implications of their gift can be understood.

The fourth characteristic of a planned gift is that there is always a *legal instrument* involved. When a donor is naming your organization in a will, estate, trust, or as a beneficiary, a legal document will set up this relationship. If there is some kind of estate transfer or transfer of physical or financial assets, all of those are conveyed with a legal instrument. This is very different than the major gifts that we might receive such as a pledge to a campaign or annual appeal responses. If we use a pledge card for these gifts, that document is a statement of intention, but it is not a legally binding agreement. When we move into the area of planned giving, the ways that those gifts are made always happen through legal instruments. Again, you will need to collaborate with legal counsel on behalf of the donor and the nonprofit to formalize this gift.

The fifth characteristic is that most planned gifts have a *deferral component.* That means that some benefit for the nonprofit or the donor is deferred to a future time. That deferral is a nice way of saying that the gift doesn't come in until the donor dies. Sometimes this is referred to as the time the gift "matures". When a donor makes a gift through a will, the nonprofit would be wise to fully acknowledge the gift as they would a check written to a capital campaign, although the nonprofit will not receive the gift until after the donor passes away.

There are other gifts such as charitable gift annuities and charitable remainder trusts that may have some immediate benefit to the nonprofit in the current lifetime of the donor but have portions of the benefit that are deferred again until they pass away. We will talk more in-depth about these types of current life and deferral gifts later in the text.

To summarize, for the purposes of our conversation there are five key components in defining a planned gift.

- It is personal. The gift is between a person and the nonprofit.
- It is structured. There are pieces and parts to it that are not common to the major and annual gifts that we are used to receiving.
- There are tax implications because this is coming from the estate or assets of a donor.

- There's a legal instrument that is involved in conveying the gift from the donor to the nonprofit.
- The gift is deferred to a future time.

Remember that donor I talked about at the beginning of the book? Let's get back to that story. In most of the following chapters I will connect the theory of the chapter with my real life donor example. When we left the story a few pages ago, I was just about to ask for the planned gift. That gift has all five characteristics mentioned in this definition. The gift was from a person. It was going to be structured. In this case, we would need to craft a gift agreement to spell out all of the moving parts of the gift. There were tax implications as this would be a charitable gift from the donor's estate. There was a significant legal instrument because the donor was amending a revocable trust to include the organization that I represented. Finally, the gift was deferred until after the donor died. However, even though we wouldn't see the gift for several years, something really special happened with that donor's annual giving. We will look at that twist a little later on.

As we explore the three basic types of planned gifts covered in this book, you will find that each of these five characteristics are accentuated in some types of gifts and perhaps not as important in others. That is a reflection of the dynamic nature of planned giving in the nonprofit world today.

CHAPTER 2

The Opportunity

The strategies outlined in this book will help you start a planned giving program no matter where your nonprofit is in its natural lifecycle with your donors. However, the ways in which we communicate the planned giving opportunity should be influenced by the generation that the donor belongs to and then customized for the donor's particular circumstance. Before we dive into strategic communication about planned giving, I think we ought to take some time to consider our audience. Each generation of planned giving prospect has had a unique experience of philanthropy. These experiences will influence their charitable giving decisions.

I have found that the motives for making a planned gift differ by generation. Also, the type of giving instrument used seems to be driven by generational attitudes. More recently, I have seen a big difference between generations in whether or not a planned gift is restricted to a particular purpose or available for general operating expenses. In the next few paragraphs I offer some reflection on what historic generational moments might influence the planned giving tendencies of the current donor generations.

The pending retirement of the baby boomers presents a historic moment in philanthropy. Most of my blogs and speeches focus on baby boomer planned giving. They do represent the greatest field of opportunity for the next influx of planned giving. However, there are really five generations of donors living today and they all have planned giving potential. These paragraphs are not meant to be an exhaustive treatment of what influences the planned giving patterns of donors. Rather, these are observations shared with me over the years by my donors. They gave me a little glimpse of what part of their upbringing guided their planned giving decision. Let's take a look at some of the characteristics and experiences that shape today's donors.

The Greatest Generation (Born 1901-1924)

This generation was born into the great prosperity of the fruits of American industrialization. The economy was healthy and jobs were plentiful. As Europe destabilized, these youngsters saw America join a battle against a far away foe with sights on western targets. World War I began right in the middle of the birth of this generation. Later, these children grew into the young adults who returned to Europe to fight for American interests. This generation saw a peaceful world torn apart during their childhood. In their adult life, they had to take a direct role in restoring global peace. They saw American prosperity turn to fear at the aggression of foreign foes. Although this generation would eventually celebrate American victory, the Great Depression also marked their worldview. The oldest of this generation were in their early adult life when the stock market crashed. The youngest were elementary age children. This economic reality left a mark on this generation's sense of financial management. These experiences shape the worldview of this generation and their sense of philanthropy.

I find that donors in this generation are very motivated to make legacy gifts that provide for community needs. During my career, some of my favorite donors in this age group were generous supporters of scholarships and youth programs. They frequently request that their gifts remain anonymous, even after their death.

The Silent Generation
(Born 1925–1945)

Some sociologists say that this generation is actually a subset of the Greatest Generation. While they share in the later part of the World War II experience with their predecessors, what sets this group apart is their childhood economic experience. These youngsters grew up during the Great Depression. They saw a kind of despair unknown in recent American history. Homes were lost, schools were closed, and jobs vanished.

In the face of this hopeless moment, this generation saw the greatest investment of the government in the domestic economy in the nation's history. The United States geared up industry to fight a two-front war. Jobs became plentiful. Prosperity was possible. Hope for a brighter financial future was almost certain. Out of the ashes of the Great Depression, the silent generation helped build a workforce that would forever change the trajectory of the American economy.

I have seen some authors refer to this generation's giving motivation to be "obligation" or "reciprocity". In other words, out of gratitude for the helps society provided in their early years, they feel a need to give to the next generation. My donors from this generation have been very interested in social service institutions, education, and care for the poor. This generation also tends to prefer anonymous giving.

Baby Boomers
(Born 1946 –1964)

They were born into the optimism of the post World War II era. The world was a safe place again, America's economy was booming, dad had a good job with a pension, and mom was at home baking pie (at least that is what was portrayed on the television). The family radio was being replaced by the television. Hope and prosperity grew in the family garden.

Meanwhile, the threat of the Communists loomed overseas. Dads and uncles who had fought in World War II had to go back into the service to fight again in Korea. While that war dampened the American spirit a bit, the prevention of Communist encroachment in South Korea was further fuel for the boomer view of America's global role and the optimism that is a part of this generation's outlook. They fought in and witnessed on television the war in Vietnam. They catalyzed one of the greatest social movements in history. Their approach to social justice on gender, race, political, and environmental fronts was revolutionary. These and other experience make this generation one of the most generous in history.

It has been fascinating to work with donors from this generation. I have found them to be more open about their giving motives. They seem very interested in understanding the impact their gift can have. Many of my baby boomer donors have been wary of large institutions and rely on personal relationships to make gifting decisions.

Generation X
(Born 1965–1979)

These are the children of the boomers and I am one of them! We grew up in a completely televised world. Our worldview was shaped by the social activism of our parents. We grew up with Reagan as President and at least part of my generation still lived under the threat of nuclear war. We saw personal computers enter the home (I still remember our Commodore 64!) and dual income families were becoming the norm. We also witnesses a global disease be described as AIDS. Our parents' stories about the Beatles and Woodstock and our grandparents stories about the European and Pacific theatres of battle were the backdrop to the development of our view of the world and informed our sense of philanthropy.

I only know of one person in my age group who has made a planned gift commitment already. It was a gift of gratitude to a hospital. As he will likely live a very long life, the hospital will not see the fruits of this gift for decades. In the meantime, though, they have a passionate advocate for their cause and that will certainly pay dividends over time.

Millennials
(Born 1980–2000)

This generation saw technology become accessible at home and at school. Cellphones were still bigger than could fit in your pocket, but computers were getting smaller and were everywhere. Their childhood was generally prosperous. This was the era of the great "dot com" expansion. They saw a war begin on live television in the Middle East and were able to watch their favorite songs turned into videos on MTV. The massive global tensions that impacted previous generations had morphed into smaller regional conflicts that seemed less ominous. Perhaps it is this lack of unifying generational narrative that makes defining this group more elusive and makes it even harder to assess their philanthropic outlook.

Understanding the narratives of the generations that came before and follow the boomers is helpful in appreciating the unique opportunity that the pending boomer retirements present to the philanthropic community.

If there was ever a time to start a planned giving program, this is it! Think about this. The last of the baby boomers turned 50 in 2014, and there are currently a 100 million adults in the United States that are over age 50. Seventy-seven million of those were born between the years of 1946 and 1964, which is the current definition of the baby boomer generation. This is a huge age group. For the first time ever they are the largest in terms of size and percentage of the U.S. population (though it looks like the millennials will catch up to with a final count of about eighty million). There hasn't ever been a generation this big.

The boomers are estimated to retire with 40 trillion dollars in assets. There's a great deal of argument about that number in the planned giving and financial advisory community. Some put it as high as 10 trillion dollars more than that. Others argue for 10 trillion dollars less. No matter what that number is, boomers are retiring with an asset base that is larger than has ever been seen in history. It is likely that baby boomers will retire earlier, live longer, be healthier, and be more active in voluntary and second careers than any generation that has come before them. There is a fabulous opportunity to engage the experience of baby boomers during their professional life in providing advice to the nonprofit community.

During retirement, many boomers are going to find volunteer service an interesting and credible way to spend some of their time. These voluntary second careers will be an awesome way of giving back based on the professional education and experiences that they had. For the first time in their lifetime, boomers are going to have more control and more freedom to explore their own personal interests and notions of charity. Nonprofits will have to create dynamic and flexible opportunities for boomers to be active and involved as volunteers, with a limited amount of time. We are expecting that boomers will spend a great deal of time in recreation activities during retirement and will want to have time-limited high-impact experiences in the nonprofit community that are flexible and outcome focused. We don't anticipate baby boomers will be motivated by recognition based on hours of service. This is a quality over quantity generation. They're going to be interested in impact and outcomes of their activity and less interested in the hours that it took to achieve the desired result.

Some studies have indicated that nearly 70% of donors plan to leave some kind of bequest, either to heirs and/ or charity, but only 5% of those over age 50 have actually made that commitment. If these numbers hold true 70 in 100 of your donors intend on making some kind of bequest commitment, but only 5 in 100 have actually taken the steps to plan their legacy. Can you imagine that in a sample of 100 of your donors who are boomers, there are 65 of them who intend to leave a charitable gift but haven't taken the steps to do that yet? That means there's great opportunity for us to engage our boomer donors in a conversation about how they might like to leave a legacy to the nonprofits they care about. There hasn't been a moment like this in the history of fundraising. There is such great potential for fruitful conversations about planned giving.

So, let's get back to my planned giving story. My donor was a boomer. I have found that donors from this generation are skeptical about large institutions. They don't have a compulsory trust of authority. This influenced the way I described the gift opportunity. It was designed to benefit a particular student group. It was not for general operating dollars. I have also noticed that boomer donors are more interested in being involved with the people that benefit from their philanthropy. That was certainly true in the case of my donor. Opportunities were created for the volunteer to provide guidance and assistance to students would eventually be beneficiaries of this philanthropic investment. Broad generalizations about donor behavior or preferences based on generational membership aren't helpful and are a potential source of trouble. However, I find that awareness of a donor's background has been helpful to me in communicating about these transformational giving opportunities.

CHAPTER 3

The Planned Giving Ecosystem

Just as we considered how the boomers relate to the generations around them, it is worthwhile to consider how planned gifts are connected to the other major charitable revenue streams. I call this the planned giving ecosystem. All the streams of fundraising have an impact on the others. They are interconnected. A change in one revenue stream will impact the rest. The greatest perceived threat to that ecosystem (and I will show that it is not a real threat) is that success one area of fundraising could hurt the others.

There is concern from time to time that planned giving will interfere with the other major forms of fundraising. Some nonprofits worry that if a donor makes a planned gift they might stop their annual or major giving after that. In my experience, planned giving tends to augment the other types of giving utilized throughout the year. Planned giving fits inside an ecosystem of other types of giving. Just as a business needs multiple streams of income to be healthy and grow, a nonprofit needs to cultivate multiple streams of fundraising support. In the next few paragraphs we'll talk about the major types of fundraising and how they directly relate to planned giving.

First, let's take a look at the annual appeal. For most nonprofits, the annual appeal takes the form of a letter or other campaign that is sent to a large group of donors at the end of the calendar year or at the end of the fiscal year. The annual appeal often includes opportunities to increase their level of giving or the campaign is focused on donor acquisition hoping to capture donors for the first time.

From time to time, some of our clients have been concerned that asking a person to make a planned gift would decrease their interest in making an annual gift. We generally find that the opposite is true. People who make a planned gift commit some part of their estate to the success and longevity of the nonprofit. They are expressing their passion for the mission of the nonprofit because of the planned gift they've made. They will want to see continued success of the nonprofit while they're still alive. This often leads to increasing their annual fund support.

If the strength and vitality of the *annual fund* is a concern of both the donor and the nonprofit, a planned gift could be constructed to support the longevity of the annual fund. A donor could direct their planned gift to be invested in an endowment, and the proceeds of that endowment are to be used for annual fund purposes each year. This is one great example of how planned gifts and annual gifts can actually work together.

Now, let's take a look at *event fundraising*. This form of fundraising happens on a periodic basis for most nonprofit clients. You might have a gala, a fashion show, a golf outing or some other event that raises money, awareness, and has an opportunity for the nonprofit to share its success and its hope for the future. Event fundraising often features event sponsorships from donors, table purchases, and silent auction contributions.

Event fundraising and planned giving can go together and are not necessarily competitive with each other. I have seen a few nonprofits use a planned gift to create a perpetual sponsorship of an event. In one case an event will be named for a family in perpetuity because of a planned gift that that family made. That gift was set up in an endowment, and that endowment will forever fund that event. For donors who have concerns, or nonprofits for that matter, that the event may not last forever, criteria can always be created in a planned gift document agreement that explains if the event will not take place for some reason that there's a secondary and even a tertiary use for the funds. Event fundraising and planned gifts can have a creative and supportive relationship to each other.

For the third type of gift we'll look at *capital campaign and major gift donations*. From time to time nonprofits will enter into a three to five year capital or major gift campaign to fund some particular need. This can be a great time to ask a donor to make a planned gift. One of the most successful gifts I ever solicited was a combination between a major gift the donor made in their current life and a planned gift that they made to benefit the institution after their death. These kinds of specific campaigns give donors an opportunity to make a big impact. They can make a lifetime major gift to provide support through current dollars and a planned gift to fund future efforts. So, of all the ways that we'll mention today, planned giving and capital or major gift campaigns have a great deal of synergy.

The last area of fundraising that we'll consider in terms of its relationship to planned giving is *special appeal giving*. In the United States there has been a big increase in philanthropy related to natural disasters. This gifts the nonprofit community an opportunity to talk with donors about making planned gifts that support these periodic appeals. People have planned gifts that they can make to respond to disasters, to respond to annual needs for the homeless or other appeals that come up in your nonprofit. Appeal giving doesn't always have to be a one-time donor experience. If a donor gives to a special appeal in your nonprofit, they could be interested in making a planned gift to future appeals of that same type.

Planned giving is part of a large ecosystem of other types of giving. When managed in harmony, these types of giving can support and augment each other. The various forms of financial support gives donors a variety of ways to share their passion with the organizations they care about. With this ecosystem as a reference point, we can now zoom in on planned giving and talk about the types of gifts that populate this aspect of giving.

My donor from the beginning of this book actually wasn't a strong annual donor when we began the planned giving conversation. He had capacity for a planned gift and interest, so that was enough for me to start the cultivation process. Once he made his gift a wonderful thing happened. His annual giving jumped dramatically! I have seen this happen so many times. Once a donor has made this transformational gift to your organization, they want to see something beneficial happen while they are still alive. This generally translates into greater volunteer involvement and financial generosity.

CHAPTER 4

The Three Basic Types
of Planned Gifts

There are several types of planned gifts from the very simple to the very complex. There are planned gift vehicles that have been around for decades, and there are new types that have only been developed in the past few years. For a nonprofit that is beginning its planned giving program, we are going to focus on three of the most often used and simplest types of planned gifts. In this chapter we'll describe how to approach a planned giving program by focusing on wills and bequests, charitable gift annuities and life insurance.

Bequests

This is the simplest way to make a substantial gift through planned giving. A bequest is communicated through the last will and testament of a donor. They can do this by giving a particular amount or a percentage of their estate to the nonprofit of their choice. This can provide tax benefits to the estate of the donor and provide a significant gift to the nonprofit that they intend to support.

A nonprofit finds out about a bequest when a donor has passed away. You get a phone call from an attorney and an estate trustee or a financial advisor to let you know that your organization was remembered in the will of one of your donors. Recently one of our hospital clients shared with us that a woman who was treated in their facility 30 years prior was so impressed with the care that she received that she left a 6-figure gift in her will to be used at the discretion of the hospital. The personal care she received during her was so impactful that she wanted to make a significant gift to the hospital for their benefit after her passing. These are the kinds of fabulous opportunities that can be created by having engaging and regular conversations with our planned gift prospects throughout the course of their life. It is quite easy for a donor to leave a percentage or a particular amount of their estate to a nonprofit. It is helpful to think back to our conversation about the impact of generational membership on planned giving. Older donors are likely to be open to the conversation about bequests, but unlikely to share their intent with you. Additionally, they are likely to request anonymity even after their death.

Some nonprofits are afraid to ask for bequests, because they are afraid that their donor will have to rewrite their will to make the gift. For the most part, this fear is unfounded. There is a document called a codicil, that is an amendment to a will that can be added as a way of changing the charitable intent of the will without rewriting the entire document. It is usually less expensive to add a codicil than it is to rewrite the entire document. It's important to note that a bequest should be acknowledged right away (via letter or personal note) once the donor has notified you of their intent or commitment. However, it's not a gift that you can count on your books as an asset because wills can be changed. We call this an intended or an expected gift, but it's not one that we would want to count, for instance, in our fundraising numbers for the year as something that we can use for budgeting purposes. We do want to steward the gift throughout the course of the donor's life and include them in special communications because of the gift, but it's not something that we should ever include in the budgeting process.

I recommend creating a legacy society for people who have left gifts in their will that you are aware of. You should develop special communications and opportunities for them to gather. This is great stewardship of the relationship and draws them closer to the organization, which reduces the possibility that the gift may change. After we ask a donor to make a gift with their will, and they agree to do that, there can be an uncomfortable moment of then asking for a copy of that documentation. This is an important conversation. There are benefits for the donor and for the nonprofit. Some donors will have peace of mind to knowing that the nonprofit understands their charitable intent. It gives you a document to enter into your formal donor database. At the time of the donor's passing you can be prepared to be in communication with attorneys, trustees and financial advisors about the transfer of the asset to your organization. I will admit, those calls are hard. I remember vividly the calls I have gotten from attorneys to let me know a beloved donor has died. Those moments are a mix of sadness and reflection. I also knew, though, that call marked the beginning of the legacy that the donor desired. I was charged with seeing that fulfilled. You won't every forget those calls and the lives that are changed because of them.

Charitable Gift Annuity

A second common form of planned gift instrument is called a charitable gift annuity. This really is one of the most fun and interesting ways that a person can make a plan gift. I offer it as one of the introductory methods because it is used so commonly and it is simple. It is not difficult to set up and it offers some very interesting benefits to the organization and to the donor. An annuity is a fixed sum of money paid to someone every year, usually for the rest of their life. A charitable gift annuity is an annuity that has been designed to make a gift to a nonprofit and to make payments on a regular basis to the donor. That's what makes it a very fascinating planned gift instrument.

Here's how it works. Let's say our donor, Mr. Smith, sets up a $10,000 charitable gift annuity with his favorite nonprofit. There will be a contract executed between the nonprofit and Mr. Smith through which he will donate $10,000, which could be cash or securities. In most cases, in that year, depending on how that donor itemizes their taxes, they'll be eligible for a federal income tax deduction.

The annuity portion comes into play because based on Mr. Smith's age, the sum he donated, and the growth of that sum as an investment, a particular amount of money will be paid to him every year from that amount for the rest of his life. Then when Mr. Smith passes away, the balance of the fund will be available to the nonprofit. The annuities are calculated on actuarial tables. So, the older a donor is, the more money they are paid on an annuity basis every year. The younger they are, the less money is available to them on an annual basis. Most annuity managers and nonprofits ask that their donors be at least age 70. Donors who are under seventy years old but older than fifty-five can sometimes take advantage of a deferred charitable gift annuity by postponing their annuity payments until a later time. There are also joint charitable gift annuities, which are really interesting because they allow payments to the donor and then payments to someone else. Annual payments are made through both lifetimes of both named persons in the annuity contract. The rates tend to be lower, but there can be some benefits when the annuitants are married.

Charitable gift annuities are really amazing planned gift instruments because they allow the donor to make a gift while they're still alive and that gift provides them some current tax benefit. It also provides them some income and provides a significant gift to the nonprofit at the death of the donor, which is the balance of the annuity. I find that these are mostly used with donors who are C-level executives or are business owners and have some level of financial sophistication. However, they are available to anyone and usually have a minimum gift amount around the $10,000 level. In terms of managing an annuity I recommend that our clients team up with a bank or a community foundation that does this on a regular basis. For organizations that are larger or grow to be larger, you can begin to manage your own charitable gift annuities. But, in the beginning, I recommend that you partner with your local community foundation or a bank to handle the annual work of stewarding the annuity. If your organization chooses to manage the gift, you are contractually responsible for the annuity payment. You have to be prepared that you may need to pay your annuitant from the principal of the gift if they outlive the expectancy of the actuarial table. By leveraging the assets of larger financial partners, like those named above, you can reduce your financial risk in a charitable gift annuity. For those of you who might be familiar with other planned giving instruments, you will recognize the CGA as the smaller younger brother of the charitable remainder trust. That is also a powerful form of planned giving that will be covered in another future book.

Life Insurance

Life insurance is a third common and very easy way for a donor to make a planned gift. There are several ways to make a gift like that possible. The first method is to use a paid-up policy or to purchase a new policy as a gift. Here's how that would work. If you have paid up the policy already you can name your favorite nonprofit as a beneficiary to a life insurance policy while still retaining ownership. When a person retains ownership they can change the beneficiary at any time so, there really isn't a tax advantage that is available in that moment. If the donor assigns a paid-up policy to a nonprofit and makes it the owner, the donor can potentially claim a federal income tax deduction for whatever the policy's fair market value is or the net of the paid premiums, whichever is less. If the premium hasn't really been paid in full, the premiums that the donor pays subsequently on behalf of the nonprofit could also be deductible. Another way to handle this is to make annual contributions directly to the nonprofit that enables the nonprofit to then pay the premiums.

Life insurance can be a really interesting and creative way to make a planned gift. It is not usually costly for the donor and certainly not for the nonprofit (as compared to charitable gift annuities which have some annual management cost). It is important to note for tax purposes that although a tax deduction can't be gained through naming a nonprofit as a primary or a contingent beneficiary, it could result in a federal estate tax deduction for the full amount of the proceeds payable to the nonprofit at the time of death which could save the estate some money. I need to add an important note here that all donors and nonprofits need to consult with their professionals about any of these gifts. This text is not designed or intended to provide tax, legal, or financial planning advice.

When a charity is named as a beneficiary of a life insurance policy a couple of really neat things happen. Since the ownership of the policy remains with the donor, their intent is completely private. Since this gift does not have to go through the probate process, it remains private even after the donor's death. This is helpful for donors for whom privacy is important, as they might not want their charitable intent to be known to their families or heirs.

A transfer of assets in an insurance contract like this is also generally incontestable. In most cases there is nobody after the death of the donor, when the estate is being liquidated, that can challenge this charitable gift. An important note for the donor and the nonprofit is that while ownership of the policy is retained by the donor while they're alive, much like wills, this isn't something that we'd want to count as an asset on the books of the nonprofit because the donor still has the ability to make a change at any time. If for some reason the donor wants to stop paying premiums but maintain a beneficiary relationship with the nonprofit, the nonprofit also has the opportunity to continue paying the premiums on behalf of the donor if it is a financially beneficial thing to do.

You can find so many types and formulations of planned gifts just by doing a simple web search. Your head will spin with the gyrations of the most advanced levels of gifts. I believe to get the fastest and most effective start to a planned giving program focusing on these three gift types, wills, charitable gift annuities and life insurance will provide the tools necessary to have an effective start with your donors. As your program grows and becomes more successful, then you can branch out into the more complex types of giving.

CHAPTER 5

Finding Potential Donors

In the nonprofit world there is a limited amount of time to spend on donor cultivation. There are so many more things to do. You have to plan events. You have to get the newsletter out. You have to pitch in answering questions at the front desk. You have to help with program delivery. How can you possibly add one more item to the fundraising to-do list like finding elusive planned giving prospects?

Finding planned giving prospects is not difficult or time consuming. If you can dedicate thirty minutes a week to planned giving, that investment could pay big dividends for the longevity of your nonprofit's mission. To help maximize your time, I have created six key characteristics that help narrow down the prospects for a planned gift. People who meet these six criteria will be the best prospects for making a planned gift to your nonprofit. Very few organizations will find that someone meets all six criteria. In my experience, the more criteria the prospective donor meets, the more likely they are to be a quality prospect. Often, someone with even 3-4 of these is someone who is worth spending time with talking about planned giving.

Criteria 1: Is the person 55 years old or older?

The first criterion is that the person is fifty-five years-old or more. This is the prime time for a planned gift donor to be thinking about how to make a legacy impact on the nonprofits that they care about. You can enter this criterion into your fundraising database, or sit down with a group of trusted advisors who can help you determine if a person falls into this age group.

This does not mean that people who are under this age are not prospects for planned giving. There are people who are forty and even thirty years-old with planned gift commitments. However, with the limited amount of time a nonprofit may have available, you will get the most return on your investment by beginning your program with people who are fifty-five years-old or more.

When you complete this search, you will end up with people falling into three generations: the boomers, the silent generation, and the greatest generation. They all require different cultivation experiences based on their generational differences. For now, simply running the query in your database ought to produce a great first list of multi-generational planned giving prospects.

Criteria 2: Gives Regularly to the Annual Fund

The second criterion to look for is someone who has been a regular part of your annual fund. The best-case scenario is someone who has been a donor for the last five years. For some of our clients, we limit it to three years of giving and for other larger clients, we look at someone who has been an annual donor for the last seven years. You can find the number that works best for you, but once you find that number, stick to that criteria and run it through your database.

You already know your best planned giving prospects. They have been giving to you for several years already. They are somebody who is actively invested in your mission. They are familiar with your programs and outcomes. There is a tendency for some nonprofits, at the beginning of their planned giving programs, to be persuaded to buy lists of people who they believe or have been led to believe by a vendor, are good planned gift prospects. This is not a good investment of your time or money. When you buy lists, you're buying lists of people who don't know you already. Within the database of your nonprofit, you already have a list of people who know you. By searching by the number of years they have been a donor to you, you increase the likelihood that they will be a great planned giving prospect.

Criteria 3: Have they given one major gift already?

A third criterion that we look at is a recent history of making a major gift. What is a major gift, you ask? I will tell you a quick story from one of my mentors who helped me with a capital campaign many years ago. We were trying to assist the client in coming up with their definition of a major gift. My mentor said this, "A major gift is like major surgery. Major surgery is anytime surgery is being done on me." He has a point! Sometimes the definition of a major gift is in the eye of the gift giver. For the sake of running a daily query in your nonprofit database, you will need to assign a number that could be equivalent to a major gift in the history of your nonprofit.

For many of our clients, this is somewhere between $5,000 and $25,000. Recently, we worked with a nonprofit whose largest individual gift has only ever been $1,000. For them, that's the definition of a major gift. For the sake of running a very clean query on your donor database, assign a major gift value that fits with your giving history and run the report. Based on how many prospects show up in the query you can adjust the value to meet your needs.

Criteria 4: Business Owners or Executives

A fourth characteristic we look at is prospects that are business owners or C level executives. A C-level is a business term that refers to someone who may be a chief executive, chief operating, chief financial, chief marketing or other chief officer in the organization. This is an important criterion in the list of planned giving prospects, because these people are likely to have assets for planned gifts. They probably have had a conversation about planned giving with their spouse or partner and would be open to a conversation about that with a nonprofit that they care about. The same is true of business owners. They have succession planning to deal with and issues related to business transference. They can be great prospects for planned giving.

There are two important items to consider here. First, this doesn't mean that planned gifts come exclusively from business owners or C-level executives. It just means that these people are more likely to make planned gifts, because of assets they may have and because the conversation may have come up in their tax planning already.

A second consideration is whether or not donor occupation is a field you use in your database. If it is unlikely that this is a criteria that you have marked in your database you may need some help asking board members for some background on potential prospects. You can also use Google to do some prospect research.

Criteria 5: Donor has No Heirs

A fifth characteristic of a planned gift prospect is a donor that has no heirs. Donors that do not have children are more likely to be planned gift donors because there isn't the second generation to which they would be committing their estate. These folks are good prospects for you to consider. My experience shows that donors without heirs tend to be legacy-minded. My non-heir prospects have been very interested in projects that support the longevity of community assets. I have found them to show particular interest in educational investments. We should be careful, though, not to assume that just because a donor doesn't have children, that would also mean there are no heirs to their estate. They could be close to a niece, nephew, or other family member who may be a beneficiary of the donor's estate plans. A healthy legacy conversation with your prospect should reveal these important details.

Criteria 6: Female and Widowed

The sixth and final prospect criterion for a planned gift prospect is someone who is a female and widowed. This is not intended to be a predatory criterion. The simple numbers tell us that women are more interested in making legacy gifts and women are more open to a legacy gift conversation. Women control more philanthropy in the United States than men, because of their longevity. For this reason, a woman, particularly a woman who is widowed, is a person who is likely to be very receptive to the planned giving conversation and interested in making a gift. It is important that we don't exploit or otherwise take advantage of this particular criterion. I have seen development officers circling retirement centers like sharks taking little old ladies out to lunch in the hopes of cultivating a gift. If this criterion is attached to a donor you already have a relationship with, you have a prospect who is in a good position to made a significant planned gift. I think it is unethical to screen prospects using this as a single criterion.

I encourage you to run these six criteria through your donor database. Any person who meets all six criteria is a prime prospect for a planned giving conversation. You can then prioritize your planned gift prospects based on the number of criteria that they meet. Those that meet more criteria you should spend the most time with. The fewer criteria a prospect meets, means your communication methods can be a little less personal until you have more time to invest. I have found, over the past several years, that these six criteria are very helpful in prioritizing the very limited time that is available to us in mid-size nonprofits.

So, how did I find the donor I mentioned at the beginning of the book? The donor was a referral from another planned gift donor and met three of the six criteria. I prefer that a prospect meet four criteria before I invest much in the cultivation process. If they meet five then we better get started right away! In this case the value of the referral outweighed the fact that the donor met so few of the criteria and I am so glad that referral came!

CHAPTER 6

The Stages of a Planned Giving Conversation

In my experience, a planned giving conversation moves through four distinct phases. I have seen these phases take as few as six weeks to be completed. I have also had donors that took years to make a planned giving decision. Like the natural progression of any relationship there is a beginning, a middle, a commitment, and if all goes well, renewal of the cycle for a lifetime. The dialogue about planned giving between the donor and development officer is truly wonderful. This is a conversation about mission, vision, and legacy. It is a conversation that is rooted in gratitude. The beginning of a planned giving conversation is the deepening of an already healthy relationship.

The Evaluation Phase: The First Meeting

Talking about an evaluation phase sounds very clinical and cold; it is anything but that. This phase is very relational. Evaluation is about determining your prospect's interest and ability in terms of making a planned gift. I prefer for this initial meeting to be brief, in a low-key atmosphere (like a coffee shop), with plenty of room for general conversation. Although this donor knows your organization, you are beginning a conversation about a new type of gift. It is like a first date in that you interact with one another in a new way. You are beginning a conversation about a legacy investment and this calls for a brief and gentle setting, not the stuffiness of a board room or over the commitment of a two-hour dinner. I like to schedule these conversations in the morning when the day is new, ideas are fresh, and there is a buzz of potential and possibility in the air! This initial meeting is to introduce the idea of planned giving and invites the prospective donor to another visit to learn more about ways of giving.

Here are a few key points and conversation starters for this meeting:

- Thank you for your support!
- You have many giving options- why have you chosen us?
- What program of ours do you care most about?
- We are starting a planned giving program to help our donors make "forever" gifts.
- Can we explain a few aspects of the program? (explain the three easy ways to give)
- Is there one of these that interests you more than the others?
- Could we visit with you in a few weeks to talk more about that method of giving?

The Cultivation Phase

This is a longer phase than the evaluation phase. You and your donor have taken a step together and agreed to explore this planned giving opportunity further. Your first meeting was brief and possibly at a coffee shop. I like to have these cultivation meetings over lunch. This time of day affords more time for discussion than a coffee visit. I have a few key restaurants that I prefer for this type of conversation. The staff is really great at picking up body language and knowing when it is a good time to check on us. This conversation introduces ways of making planned gifts and how those gifts can be used to further the mission of your organization. Lunch represents a little more commitment than the coffee meeting but not quite the level of involvement of a meeting later in the day. This layout for the second meeting will likely result in several more meetings of this type. Some planned giving decisions can lead to a gift commitment in eighteen to twenty-four months. I don't want to give the impression that it is an easy four-step process. Instead, I hope to show the progression of the meetings as stages of relationship development; not boxes that are checked along the way. However many visits this stage takes, it should always end with a request by you to your donor for permission to create a planned giving proposal. If they agree, that is the key indicator you are ready for the last step.

Here are a few key points and conversations starters for this meeting:

–   Thank you for making time for us!

- Last time we were together you mentioned that (X) part of our program was really important to you
- You also said that (Y) method of planned giving was interesting to you
- Can we share a few ways you could make a gift like that?
- bring an example of a codicil (amendment to a will)
- bring an example of how whole and term life could be used
- bring an illustration of the impact of a charitable gift annuity
- With a gift like this you could have a lasting impact on (our mission, programs, services)
- What questions do you have?
- Would you like to consider setting up a gift like this?

The Solicitation Phase

This is the moment we have been waiting for! After carefully listening to the donor's passion and matching up their planned giving needs with opportunities to further the mission of your organization, you are ready to present a proposal. This is the culmination of your work! My best presentations have been over dinner. It is a great time of day. You and your donor have an opportunity to reflect on your journey, review the proposal and talk about next steps. Dinner meetings represent the most commitment of time and money to the donor relationship. It can be an ideal time to talk about a gift proposal. Again, it is important to be at a restaurant with wait staff who are used to business meetings so that you aren't interrupted at an inopportune time.

In the previous phase, you asked permission to ask for a gift. Now, you get to make the actual ask! Before you present the proposal it is always good to ask these questions as a quick reality check:

- As I recall, you are really fond of our XYZ program. Is that right?
- And you think that we could improve the program by doing PDQ?
- I have prepared for you a proposal that outlines how we can make those improvements. Can we review it together?

I also love this last question because solicitation (asking for the gift) is a collaborative process. The solicitor and the donor create the gift together in the best of circumstances. When the donor has a role in reviewing and editing *their own gift proposal*, everyone wins!

The Stewardship Phase

In some ways, the real work of planned giving starts *after* the gift commitment has been made. Like all long-term relationships, maintaining connection, gratitude, and growth between the peak moments, is important.

We shouldn't treat our donors like ATMs. We can't just show up when we need money. We need to have intentional conversations about stewarding our donor relationships. In some circles of fundraising, this phase is called "Follow Up". I even used that term at one point in my career. I don't anymore. That phrase sounds like a process or a box that has to be checked after a gift.

Stewardship is much more than follow-up. It is about a gift that has been made, it is about offering gratitude for that gift, and it is about the joyful sharing of the fruits of that gift. It is an awesome phase of a relationship with a donor.

Here are a few key responsibilities in this phase of the relationship.

As soon as a planned gift commitment is completed, send a handwritten note to the donor. Few gestures in modern correspondence are as impactful as a handwritten note. Yes, you can send your standard form letter. However, putting your pen to paper will send a strong message about the personal value of this relationship.

It is likely that you met with your donor at regular intervals leading up to the gift being made. Well, don't stop getting together! Yes, you only have so much time. Yes, your donors are busy people, too. But, let's say you may have been meeting every four to six weeks leading up to the gift. When the gift came in you sent a handwritten note. Your formal thank you letter probably went out a week later. So, go ahead and set up a short meeting about twelve to eighteen weeks out to give a brief update on your planned giving program, the growth of your organization, or your plans for the following year.

Have a beneficiary send a note. If the donor gave to a scholarship, try to get a recipient to send a handwritten note to the donor. If they funded a new outreach program, see if a participant can send a note. If they funded a new piece of equipment, perhaps a user can pen a short thank you note. You get the idea. Donors hear from you fairly often.

Hearing from someone who benefits from their gift can be very impactful.

Be transparent about reporting. A few years ago I had a donor make a gift to a scholarship fund. That year, there were no students who met the scholarship criteria. Sharing that news was tough. Their gift really didn't get used and I felt terrible about it. However, it gave me a great opportunity to have a conversation about expanding their scholarship criteria.

Start getting ready for the return of your relationship to phase one. By this point, you have done an excellent job keeping the donor informed about the effects of their gift. Congratulations! You have thanked them, listened to their interests and involved them in your mission. Now it is time to starting circling around to the first phase of the donor cycle! You have reached that great moment where you and the donor begin to start considering how their passion connects to another possible investment in the great work you are doing.

Over the last few pages I have shared the times and places that seem to be optimal for planned giving conversations. I have also had successful meetings in the homes of donors and on the golf course. Rarely do these meetings go well in an office setting. I have had some great successes and colossal failures in donor stewardship. If you are attentive to your donor and authentically steward the relationship, you both will establish a healthy rhythm of getting together between gifts.

With my donor from the beginning of the book, this whole process took about eighteen months. I have found this to be a little faster than average. I have had some conversations take up to three years from initial contact to solicitation. One gift was committed in less than six months (that is not usual at all). Over the course of these eighteen months, we probably met six times with calls and correspondence in between. That worked in the rhythm of this relationship with this donor. You will find what will work best for you and your donors.

CHAPTER 7

Your Planned Giving Committee

I have tried to demonstrate that the steps and processes thus far are fairly straightforward and could be accomplished with just a little time each week. However, there is no reason to row the planned giving boat all by yourself. While those who have dedicated their lives to nonprofit work are heroes, to be really successful, they understand they can't do it alone. We need to build a team around us to be successful. That's why I think it's important that any nonprofit that begins a planned giving program ought to have a committee backing them up. First let's take a look at what the planned giving committee does and then we'll talk about who should be on it.

The first role of a planned giving committee is to help you identify prospects. Without potential donors, you don't have a program! The best way to start that process is to put together a list of prospects from your database based on the criteria explained in chapter five. The planned giving committee can help you prioritize those prospects and maybe even add a few that didn't come out of your data query.

A committee can be invaluable in gathering some qualitative data about when potential donors might be more open to planned giving conversations. Another great contribution that a committee can offer is suggesting new prospects that didn't turn up in our research. Keep in mind that if a committee member suggests a name that isn't currently on your donor list, then expect the relationship development period towards a planned giving gift to take longer than a current donor. We should willingly invest the time in our committee's recommendations as they often know these individuals personally and professionally.

The second role of the planned gift committee is to assist in securing planned gifts. Because of their relationships in the community, your committee members can begin conversations with donors that sometimes we can't. The committee members are often peers of planned gift donors and they're in the position to talk about legacies in the way that many of us as staff are not able to. As development officers and staff we have a key role in conducting the entire symphony of nonprofit fundraising. From annual gifts, to events, to major gifts, and beyond, we are responsible for it all. We serve our organization and our donors best when we have the right person making the ask and that isn't always you and me. The committee can play a key role in getting the door open for a conversation and can often be the right person to solicit the gift.

The third important role of a planned gift committee is to be a part of developing an annual communication plan. That communication plan will include how we communicate planned gift opportunities through newsletters, the annual report, awareness events and regular direct communication with planned gift prospects and planned gift donors. This process is covered in the next chapter.

The fourth important role of the planned gift committee is to lead by example. Members of our planned gift committee should consider and be encourage to make a planned gift through their will, through a charitable gift annuity, life insurance or a vehicle they may already have available to them such as a trust. By making a planned gift they're in a better position to have a conversation with their peers about their interest in making a gift.

The last role of the committee is that they should meet on a regular basis. For new gift committees this may mean as often as once a month. For more established committees, quarterly meeting is advisable and later in the life cycle of the planned gift committee they may only need to meet twice a year.

This brings us to another important question, who should be on the planned gift committee? The people who populate this committee represent a cross section of the organization as donor base and the expertise required to be effective in this realm of planned gift fundraising. Here are a few of the people that ought to be considered for membership on this committee:

I believe the CEO of the nonprofit organization should be a part of this committee at least initially. If a planned giving program is new to your organization, you will have to consider investments in terms of the human capital of the organization plus some financial investment of printed resources and video resources to communicate about planned giving and for that reason having the chief executive of the organization on board is critically important.

If you haven't done so already, you need to decide which staff officer will be in charge of the planned giving program. This person needs to be on the committee. This person doesn't have to be a planned giving expert. This person just needs to have the passion to share the story and the opportunity of planned giving with donors.

The third important person to have on the committee would be either the current attorney of the nonprofit or a volunteer attorney in the community who would be interested in providing advice. It's important to have some legal guidance as you begin your planned gift program. Later on, you might develop a seminar around how to make wills as a planned giving vehicle. An attorney will be a great partner in these outreach and education efforts.

It's good to have a CPA on this committee. Sometimes that could be the CPA that provides services for the nonprofit or it could be a CPA who is a community volunteer. Because of the tax implications of planned gifts, it's important to invite one of these professionals to assist your organization. It would also be good to have somebody from your community foundation and or a local bank that may provide assistance in managing endowments or charitable gifts annuities on your behalf. These people provide valuable resources and perspectives that would make the work of the planned gift committee much more effective.

I do encourage you to have a representative of the boomer generation on your committee. This would be a person who would have met many of the criteria for being a prospective planned gift donor. They could be there to offer advice on how your materials would be received by boomers.

I would encourage you to have someone from the generation just older than the boomers also on the committee to provide some valuable perspective. They will have insights about their peers and be able to review materials that you might send to prospects. One of our clients engaged a member of the silent generation on their committee. The staff had proofed and printed a draft of their first planned giving brochure. This experienced committee member remarked, "I am sure this is very good, but the print is too small!" This helpful comment was the catalyst for a large font version of the brochure! I also encourage you to have a young professional on the committee because they will be the next generation of active committee members. This is good nonprofit leadership succession planning. I have also seen some younger committee members make substantial planned gifts using life insurance products.

Lastly, I do want to make sure that our committees are gender and race inclusive. When we look at some of the descriptors of the people that we talked about just a moment ago in terms of attorneys, CPAs and financial advisors, some of those roles are traditionally filled by men. It is important that we have a very good representation of women on the planned gift committee because the way that they receive and process information about legacy giving is different than men. Missing their input would be a loss in a planned giving committee. We also want our committees to be ethnically inclusive, if you have ethnic populations in your donor based that will be communicated with about the planned giving opportunity. It's important to make sure they're included in the committee so that cultural norms from their ethnicity can be included in the way planned giving is discussed and offered as a giving opportunity.

The planned giving committee is a resource of information and human capital to effectively share the legacy opportunity with your potential donors. Their support and feedback is a critical component of long-term success. A sample job description for this committee is included in the appendix of this book.

CHAPTER 8

Communication and Planned Giving

Building awareness of your planned giving program is an important strategy for your success. There are several methods that you should explore to communicate to your prospects about your planned giving program. Keep in mind that it may take several impressions before a donor is ready to respond and that those impressions my come through several communication vehicles. Like your relationship with your donor, communicating about planned giving opportunities take time and patience.

Postal Letter

The first method is to use the traditional postal letter. Although mail open rates are dropping among boomers and the generations that came before them, it is still a good practice to offer an introductory letter, perhaps with a brochure that describes why you are beginning your planned gift program. There are at least three elements that ought to be included in this letter.

Open the letter with a paragraph about the current success of your nonprofit, the things that you have achieved, the milestones, and the outcomes that you have to celebrate. Continue the letter with a description about your plans for future program growth. Describe your growth opportunities in terms of mission, services, and impact. Show how respond to community needs by providing valuable programs and outreach. Conclude your letter with a description of how your planned giving program will make that possible. Legacy gifts provide sustaining gifts that are investments in the future. A sample letter is included for you in the appendix of this book.

Email

The second method you'll want to consider is how to communicate a planned gift program via email. If you think about the amount of email that you send and receive, including some planned giving language at the end of an email might be the subtle trigger that moves a donor to call you about an opportunity for a gift. You might consider something like, "Have you considered making a gift through your will or bequest? For more information on this opportunity, click here or call this number" That kind of language ought to be added to the footer of all of your emails to increase awareness about your new planned giving program. Some research indicates that boomers have much higher electronic engagement rates than expected.

Annual Report

The third communication method is through your annual report. Hopefully all nonprofits these days are preparing a report at the end of their financial year and certainly at the end of their calendar year for donors to understand what money came in and how it was used. This offers a great opportunity to talk about legacy giving. Those annual reports should always include success stories of program impact over the previous year and a vision story or two about the directions you are headed in the year to come. You should include a quote or two from people who have already made a legacy gift. It is also helpful to list the name, phone number or an email address of a staff member when a prospect is ready to begin this conversation. Peer validation is a powerful motivator in giving decisions. Since your annual fund readership is likely generationally diverse, you will want to include planned giving success stories from multiple generations to increase the likelihood of increasing someone's interest through peer validation.

Awareness Event

The fourth way to communicate about your planned gift program is through what I call an awareness event. This is one of my favorite communication methods because planned giving is very personal as compared to the level of donor interaction we have with an annual gift. Because of how personal it is, I believe we ought to communicate about planned giving face to face as much as possible. An awareness event is often held in the home of a board member or a current planned gift donor. Your invitation list includes members of the board, your committee, and planned gift prospects. The program for the afternoon or evening is very simple:

- arrival and greeting by the chair of the board or the CEO of the non profit
- time for socializing and visiting
- Brief story by someone who has made a planned gift encouraging others to begin that conversation with the non profit
- conclude the evening with the board chair or CEO offering thanks for everyone that attended and then as everyone left, you would deliver your planned gift brochure to all the attendees

These kind of awareness events spark conversation, build connections, and offer you an opportunity to open a door with people in a very non threatening way about the possibilities of making a legacy gift.

Mobile Technologies

Some newer ways to talk about planned giving harness the product of technology. Baby boomers are increasingly spending time on the internet. A good number of them have mobile phones and are consuming mobile content, so we ought to meet them where they are by using those same technological vehicles. One of the ways I suggest to communicate is through a YouTube (or Vimeo) video. YouTube subscription rates are skyrocketing. People are consuming videos online almost more than they consume them through traditional video media. Creating a video is not a difficult thing to do. It is a matter of taking what might be your short presentation, and offering that in front of a laptop or using a local video professional to put together a video. It should be three or four minutes that essentially describe the same things that you would describe in your letter, in your annual report, or your awareness event. Where has your organization been in terms of success? Where would you like to be in terms of growth and how can planned giving make that possible? This video doesn't need to be anything more than four to six minutes. This is not an Emmy award winning production. It's something that is brief, content rich and digestible. It can be uploaded to the internet and available to be watched anytime a donor has an interest. You can share the links to your video on your website, social media pages, and on your email campaigns.

Webinars

Another communication platform to consider using is a webinar. Webinars used to be pretty complicated to produce. But today they are easier than ever. A webinar responds to the needs of boomers by delivering content in a way that is engaging, quick and efficient, and not location-specific. There are multiple affordable platforms that allow you to reach hundreds of people at a time using a PowerPoint-style presentation. Consider the difficulty of gathering people for meetings or at particular locations for events. Using a webinar you can offer a dozen opportunities in a week to people all across the country and reach larger audiences than you ever could physically. It gives us an opportunity to share our story, talk about partnership opportunities, and operate a call to action for a next step for our prospects. You could pretty easily put together a webinar for boomers in your donor database or in your sphere of influence. If you are using slides for presentations or for creating your annual report, you can break that information down into a few slides for your webinar. Next, you select a webinar platform and send out an email invitation to people that you think would be interested. This is a great and very flexible way for people to interact with your planned giving content and you program.

Webinars can also be recorded which allow people to consume your content even after the presentation so that not every opportunity has to be live. One of the great things that I love about webinars is that people can ask questions anonymously. I have found some times that more questions are asked in webinars than are in face to face presentations. Because boomers have adopted emerging technologies so readily, I would highly encourage considering the use of webinar to stay in contact with your donors and prospects about planned giving opportunities.

Podcasts

These on-demand audio broadcasts have really taken off over the past few years. With a laptop and a microphone, you can be on the way to creating a podcast for your nonprofit. It is as simple a recording a conversation with a board member, a donor, volunteer, or staff member. The topics could range from your organization's impact, to your plans for a growth, or a look at your history. Once you sign up with a podcasting service, you can offer a digital library for your prospects and donors to interact with at any time. If you want your podcast to have a more sophisticated feel, you can hire an outside producer who can add music and do some editing for you. I expect that podcast listenership will increase among baby boomers. This will be a great new way to build a relationship with them!

You have a great story to tell. Your nonprofit has done impactful work that has changed lives. You owe it to those you serve to tell your story to potential donors in a compelling way. You owe it to your potential donors to offer them a way that they can enrich the lives of others. You are the matchmaker who brings the two together. Communicating that opportunity is a rich a powerful experience. Go for it!

CHAPTER 9

Measuring Your Results

If you have experience in major gift fundraising you know that we always have an overall goal we try to achieve and an ask amount for each potential donor. This makes it fairly easy to measure success based on the amount raised at any given point on the fundraising calendar. This kind of measurement in harder in planned giving.

Over the years, I have been asked many times, "How much are we trying to raise with this planned giving program?" It's a fair question based on the experiences that people have had with major gift fundraising, but misguided when applied to planned giving. Here is where I think the question is coming from and how we go about answering it.

Isn't This Like Every Other Type of Giving?

Well, actually, no. Many of our volunteers have sat on major gift, annual fund, or event committees. In those modes of fundraising there is a prospect list, an ask amount, a solicitor, and a timeline on which we need the gift to be made. It is fairly easy to measure success because "the ask" is specific and time driven. For instance, consider a major gift team that needs to raise just over $2 million in 10 months and has a prospect list of around 300 contacts. We will be able to measure success fairly easily because we can track them on a monthly basis against their goal and timeline. Because of the uniqueness of how planned gifts are requested and fulfilled, these types of metrics don't fit very well.

Most Nonprofits Get it Wrong

This is more direct than I prefer to be. The reality is that many nonprofits think they have a planned giving program and they really don't. I have seen it too many times: they convene a committee of the best and brightest, they put a nice little blurb in the newsletter and on their pledge cards about making planned gifts. They may have even sent out a letter or brochure. And then they waited. And waited some more. And nothing happened. They spent all that time, energy, and resources without much (if any) return. I call this "passive planned giving". It has a role as a component of a comprehensive planned giving program, but a planned giving program it does not make! This approach creates a little awareness, but does little to inform donors of any opportunity. This approach certainly doesn't fit the bill of a personal invitation to make a planned gift. Every time I hear someone say, "We tried planned giving and it didn't work" I ask them what they tried and they tell me about the passive program described above. Their frustration with a failed process can lead them to want to give up on planned giving altogether.

So How Do We Measure Success?

Over the years I have developed some metrics that demonstrate the return on passive and active elements of a comprehensive planned giving program. While passive programming elements don't result in a successful program, they are a part of an intelligent holistic approach to planned giving. Here are my recommended metrics for a comprehensive planned giving program:

Number of impressions- This is the sum total of the number of times a prospect could see your planned giving materials. So, if a donor received your annual report, your monthly e-newsletter, an annual pledge card, and a separate mailer on planned giving, that donor would have fifteen impressions if all those communication pieces had something about your planned giving program. It is important to note that these are possible impressions, not actual impressions. We don't know if they read the whole annual report or opened the e-newsletter. That is one reason why this is an ineffective way to try to build a planned giving program. However, as part of a holistic approach, this impression measurement tool can help you tell your planned giving story with more frequency.

Number of Inquiries- So, on all of those materials mentioned above you had a little box somewhere that says something like, "Yes, I would like more information on planned giving." At some point, with enough impressions you are likely to get a few inquiries. This number of inquiries stands alone as a metric but can also be divided by the number of impressions to get a conversion ratio. Using the example above, there were fifteen total times in that year that a donor could have seen some information on your planned giving program. If you have one hundred donors, multiply that by the number of times you communicated about your planned giving program and you find your total impressions were fifteen hundred. If you got two inquiries, that would be a .13% conversion. That won't build a program, but it is a beginning.

Number of Solicitations- This is where we start to move into an active planned giving program! The fun begins here! The best programs actually get in front of prospects and ask them to consider a planned gift. You will notice your conversation ratio leap way above the passive program once you start doing this. The more face-to-face asks you can make, the more commitments you will get! The passive program shared the opportunity and sits back and hopes the phone will ring. The active program sends out the information and picks up the phone! I believe even the smallest nonprofit organization can make two planned giving calls a week. Based on the criteria of a potential donor, they know you already. This is an old friend, not a new relationship. Some of my best planned giving visits have only lasted thirty minutes and some have even happened on the phone!

Number of Gifts- This gets to be really interesting. When you sit face-to-face with a donor and ask them to include your organization in their will you have just offered the opportunity for your donor to leave a lasting legacy. It is an amazing moment! However, the way these gifts get solicited is different than we are used to. In major gift fundraising the ask often sounds like this, "Rob would you consider a gift of $100,000 over the next three years for our capital campaign?" and being able to follow up on the amount and timeline. In planned giving, the ask looks different. It might go like this, "Rob, would you consider leaving a (specific amount or percentage) of your estate to our organization to continue our work in the community?" Notice that there isn't a timeline on the gift. Planned gift donors have longer decision cycles. So, stewardship is softer than a major gift ask. In follow up you might say, "Rob, for record keeping purposes, we are taking note of donors who are including us in their estate plan. Are you interested in sharing your plans with me?" This is a delicate question. You will know if it is appropriate for your relationship with your donor. If they agree, this allows you to record the expectancy of a gift at some future time. With this type of dialogue you can get a sense of how many planned gifts could be on the horizon at some future time.

Amount of Gifts- Because of the type of planned giving vehicles we use (from wills, trusts, insurance, annuities, securities) some of their values can fluctuate. Knowing that a donor has left thirty percent of their estate to you in their will is nice, but you don't really know the value of their estate now and it will likely change over time. However, there are ways to gently ask if specific amounts have been named in a will, or if a life insurance policy has been gifted to you. You can also estimate remainder amounts for annuity gifts. Trying to determine the amount of planned gifts that you have in your expectancy pipeline is tough, but some committee members need that number out there as a motivational factor. We owe it to them to generate an estimate. It is always important to note that these amounts, even charitable gift annuities, should not be considered for future budgets. There are too many fluctuating variables. Record the expectancy and only budget when the gift has matured.

When you start your program, you can create your own metrics so you can start to measure return on investment for your efforts. Planned gifts are a little longer and a more nuanced process than major gifts, but the conversations and legacy impact are larger than you might have ever experienced.

With seventy-seven million boomers retiring over the next thirty years with forty trillion in assets, we need to get moving now to create *active planned giving programs* to invite the support of this important generation of donors. We can generate metrics all day long to measure effectiveness but let's not spend so much time on measurement that we lose time getting in front of our donors and inviting their legacy support.

EPILOGUE

We have been on quite a journey together over the past few pages. From gifts types, to forming a committee, to finding prospects, I hope this text is helpful to you. I hope you found enough here to get you started in the wonderful world of planned giving. This is the most exciting field of philanthropy today and it will be for decades to come. It has been my joy to try to get some practical tips and strategies on paper so that you can get started.

I feel like I owe you a conclusion about my meeting with my donor. Remember, the day was cold and we were just weeks from the holidays. We had been meeting for about eighteen months. I didn't have the benefit of a book like this. I didn't have formal fundraising education. It was my first planned gift solicitation. The donor was a few minutes late, which only increased my anxiety. Finally, our breakfast arrived and we began our conversation. A wonderful thing happens when you spend time on planned giving. You get to learn about a person's life. You have the honor of getting to learn about their desired legacy. You form a substantive relationship. You, the professional fundraiser, take on the commitment of stewarding another person's transformational investment in your nonprofit. At what seemed like the right time, I said, "It has been a honor to get to know you over the past several months. I feel like I have a clear understanding of the impact you want to make. Are you ready to make a planned gift commitment to our organization?" The question floated across the table and seemed to hang there. I am sure I garbled a few of the words. I really didn't know what would happen next. The donor looked back at me and said, "It's the right time to do this." Wow! In my head fireworks were going off! On the outside I tried to keep my composure and look like I had done this a hundred times before. I honestly don't remember what happened after that. I know it took a few weeks to get the paperwork done (remember the donor was amending a trust and I had a gift agreement to prepare). After that experience, I knew that I wanted planned giving to be a big part of my career. I am so thankful for that day.

I truly believe the quote by Dr. King that I shared at the beginning of the book. You don't have to see the whole staircase, you just have to take the first few steps. In planned giving the first step is simple. Sit down with a current annual donor and ask, "Can we have a conversation about your legacy with our organization?" that is a mystical and wonderful moment in the field of fundraising. After reading this book, you are ready to ask that question of donors who already invest in the good work you are doing.

It has been an honor for me to work in the field of planned giving and an even greater honor to share what I know with you. We get to change lives and communities one gift at a time. Please feel free to let me know how I can help you on this amazing journey.

Rob Henson, CFRE

APPENDIX

Frequently Asked Questions

This section addresses some common concerns that come up when a nonprofit begins a planned giving program. These questions come up nearly every day in our practice.

Is my nonprofit too new to start a planned giving program? Sometimes clients or their donors have expressed a concern about making a planned gift to a young nonprofit. The question often looks like this, "What happens to a planned gift if the organization doesn't exist when the gift matures?" It is a good question and it deserves a thoughtful answer. There are mechanisms to provide some assurances to the donor. When a person makes a planned gift and there's some concern about the stability or longevity of the nonprofit, the donor has the option to name a successor organization.

For example: let's say that a donor wants to make a gift to ABC charity. ABC has only been around for about five years. The donor has some concern about the long-term sustainability of ABC. The donor has the opportunity to add a sentence in their gift agreement that says if ABC Charity is no longer operating at the time the gift is conveyed, then XYZ Charity becomes a beneficiary of this gift. That should answer concerns that donors have about organizational stability in terms of planned giving.

Do we have enough donors to start a planned giving program? There isn't a minimum number of prospects to start a planned giving program. If you have donors, you have planned giving prospects. Even an organization that may only be five years old will have prospects in their donor population that could be making planned gifts. You have an awesome opportunity to offer your donors multiple ways of supporting your mission. Whether you have 50 or 5,000 donors, you can reach out to anyone who meets the prospect criteria to begin a conversation about their legacy.

Will planned gifts reduce other types of giving? For those of you who skipped to this section of the book, I cover this issue in Chapter 3. My experience is that planned giving does not compete with annual, current, or pledged gifts. It actually augments giving. Planned giving donors many times will increase their annual giving, because they know that the benefit of their planned gift is something they'll never see, and so they would like to see while they are alive their funds being put to good use in the organization that they care so much about, that they've left them in their estate plans. They like to be a part of their success today.

More often than not, I see that planned giving donors tend to increase their annual support. I also find that planned gift donors tend to make larger capital campaign and major gift investments. The average planned gift is $35,000 in the United States when they are unsolicited, and the solicited planned gift can as much as five or ten times that. I find that planned gift donors increase their volunteer engagement, are higher annual fund donors, larger major gift donors, and passionate advocates for your nonprofit once they have made their planned gift commitment.

Organizations need not worry that they're going to lose money today for the benefit of getting money tomorrow.

Is this too complicated for us? I cover this in some detail in Chapter 1. Many nonprofits worry that planned giving is just too complicated for their staff to handle. Nonprofits can fall into the trap of believing that planned giving is only the domain of major universities and hospitals, and that you have to have a law degree or a similar degree to solicit planned gifts. That is just not true. Most planned giving is actually quite simple.

There are a few products that are very complex, but product knowledge isn't the primary responsibility of the organization that is soliciting the planned gift. Our primary responsibility in fundraising is stewardship of our relationship with our donor. When we steward that relationship well, we know what our donor's giving needs are, and our donor knows what our growth aspirations are in our nonprofit. Then we are able to offer our donor ways of making gifts that improve the outcomes that we both care about.

A gift solicitor doesn't need to know how to write a will or how to amend a will using a codicil. A gift solicitor is responsible for beginning the legacy giving conversation with a potential donor. As the conversation progresses, the gift solicitor will offer the opportunity to help their donor find someone who can turn their charitable intent into a written plan.

If you simply focus on the three basic planned giving types outlined in this book: wills and bequests, life insurance, and charitable gift annuities you will be able to discuss over 80% of planned gifts that you will ever encounter. When a donor happens to mention that they might like to make a gift using some kind of charitable remainder or charitable lead trust, you will be able to quickly refer to the attorney that takes care of your nonprofit's legal matters or a volunteer attorney on your board or planned giving committee who will be able to help carry the ball with you from there.

I don't want lack of legal or accounting knowledge to prevent nonprofits from beginning healthy conversations with our donors about making planned gifts, and then feeling confident enough to loop in professionals when the time is right to help meet the needs of donors.

Will planned giving take too much staff time? It should not. I am not suggesting that you start a new department. I am suggesting that someone on staff takes the responsibility to query a list of potential donors, round up a committee of professional advisors, and methodically begin legacy conversations with current donors that have great potential to make planned gifts. I started by spending just thirty minutes a week on planned giving. It certainly paid off.

How much will it cost to have a planned giving program? You will have some printed materials, some cultivation visits with prospects, and perhaps a small event. Considering the average unsolicited bequest is $35,000, I think you will find a modest investment in quality donor conversations will pay dividends to the mission of your organization.

Where do I find the millionaires I read about in the newspaper? I cringe every time there is a story in the paper about a widowed schoolteacher that just left millions to her favorite charity. Two things happen after that article is printed: 1) clients want to know why I didn't know about her and 2) clients want to know how to find more donors like her! The metrics of planned giving tell us that the criteria outlined in Chapter 5 are the best guide to finding planned giving donors. Finding and chasing down these unicorn donors you read about in the paper is a fool's errand. You may find one or two prospects like this in a query of your database, but they are rare. You already know your best prospects.

Potential Elements of the Planned Giving Brochure

Intro letter from Executive Director- this letter shares a brief overview of the organization, describes the current successes of the mission, and the future hopes for growth and effectiveness. This letter should feature a picture of the Executive Director and be about three paragraphs.

Testimonial from beneficiary- this paragraph is written by or for someone who has benefitted from the organization. If they are able/willing to be named and photographed, that is ideal. The tone of this section is gratitude for the generosity of donors and the impact that their gifts make. A picture is preferable if permitted by your agency.

Testimonial from planned giving donor- this paragraph is written by or for someone who has already made a planned gift. If they are able/willing to be named and photographed, that is ideal. The tone of this section reflects the good feelings of the donor about making their gift. Getting this section done requires someone to be an early or initial donor. Generally this is a member of the Board or planned giving committee. A picture of the donor makes this part of the brochure more personal for the reader.

Description of Types of Gifts- this section describes the types of gifts you will generally offer to donors. I suggest you start with wills, CGAs, and basic life insurance products. You only need basic descriptions in this section. It can be tempting to get into details, but that isn't the point of the brochure and could be distracting to the reader.

Concluding Gratitude Paragraph- this can be written by a member of the Board or other high profile volunteer. This paragraph welcomes the reader to further consideration and conversation about planned giving. The end of this paragraph should provide staff contact information.

Initial Planned Giving Interest Letter

Dear First/Supporter,

I am thankful for your support of and interest in (name of organization).

Because of your generosity, (name of organization) has the resources to transform and strengthen the lives of young people and their families. We are the only organization that provides (insert your mission and services here).

I would like to invite you to take a look at some ways of extending your legacy and impact so that the good work you have started/contributed to will continue for generations to come.

I have included some materials that explain the basics of our new planned giving program. I hope we can consider this as a beginning of a fruitful conversation about your role in the future work of (name of organization).

I hope that you find this information helpful. Please feel free to reach out to me (include contact info) if you have any questions. It would be an honor to visit with you about this opportunity.

I am grateful for your partnership in our mission. I am looking forward to discussing how we can expand your impact on our work.

With gratitude,

Executive Director

PLANNED GIVING COMMITTEE
JOB DESCRIPTION

The (name of organization) Planned Giving Committee cultivates planned gifts to secure resources that support and further the mission, program, and outcomes of (name of organization).

Bequests will likely be the gift vehicle of choice for many donors, but other gift vehicles such as gift annuities and life insurance will be encouraged as well.

The role of the committee is to:

- Identify potential planned gift donors
- Cultivate relationships with potential donors
- Assist the staff in soliciting planned gifts commitments
- Contribute to the creation of the annual communication plan
- Lead by example through considering their own planned gift
- Meet at least quarterly

The staff of (name of organization are committed to provide timely meeting agenda, updates on gift commitments (when appropriate), collateral support for cultivation/solicitation meetings, and assistance in making prospect visits when needed.

_____

Executive Director

I, _____ am
committed to being an active member of this committee.
I will consider my own planned gift which will give me
credibility in cultivating other prospects. I will assist in
identifying and cultivating potential planned gift donors. I
will actively look for opportunities for our planned giving
program to be marketed in the community.

_____

Planned Giving Committee Member

Sample Agenda for Planned Giving Committee Kick-Off Meeting

Welcome

- Thank you for making the time to be a part of this important effort
- A Planned Giving strategy is the next great step in our development plan
- We all know that $41 trillion is about to hit the market with the boomer retirement
- Nonprofits that have the infrastructure to ask for gifts will benefit from this wave
- We have created a plan that we would like you to be a part of

Our Strategy

- We have identified (NUMBER) of prospects who are likely planned giving donors
- They meet a number of key criteria including: age, years of support, amount of support, business success, and known legacy opportunities.
- We have a three step plan to introduce them to our planned giving strategy

The Plan

- Intro letter and brochure mailed to prospects
- Cultivation event in November
- Personal visits following cultivation event

Our Outcomes Today

- Your thoughts on the brochure
- Input on the cultivation venue
- Your commitment to help with personal visits

Planned Giving Program Calendar

Month	Outcome
June	Program Planning
July	Brochure Copy
	Calendar
	Prospect List
	Committee Description
	Committee List
August	Brochure Draft
	Committee Orientation
September	Passive invite starts
	Awareness Event Planning
	Awareness Event invite mailed
	Ask training for staff
October	Awareness Event
	Letter to prospects
	First prospect visits
Nov-Dec	Visits Continue
January	Assess Strategy and Results

General Calendar Suggestions

2 Letters per Year to Prospects

2 Articles per Year in Newsletter

2 Small Awareness Events per Year

www.ingramcontent.com/pod-product-compliance
Lightning Source LLC
Chambersburg PA
CBHW030906180526
45163CB00004B/1726